THE **BIG** TIME

TAYLOR LAUTNER

VALERIE BODDEN

CREATIVE EDUCATION

THE BIG TIME

TAYLOR LAUTNER

TABLE OF CONTENTS

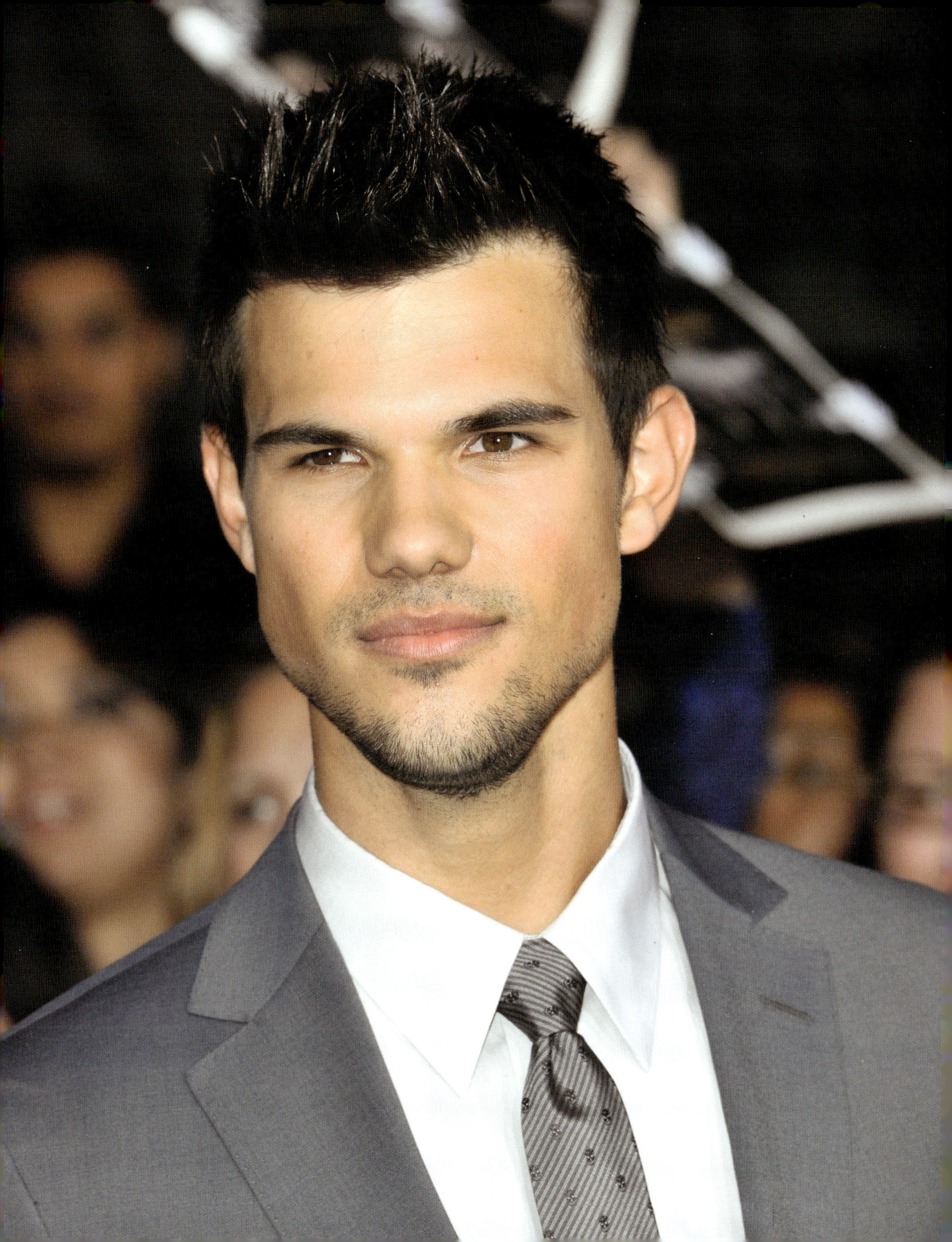

E
LG

MEET TAYLOR

It is 4:00 in the morning. Taylor steps off a plane. He thinks he will have a quiet day. Then he is met by hundreds of cheering fans. This is the greeting Taylor gets all around the world!

Taylor Lautner is an actor. Fans know him best for his role in the *Twilight* movies. Many people think Taylor is one of the best young actors today.

Taylor has filmed movies in places like Washington, New York, and Canada.

TAYLOR'S CHILDHOOD

Taylor was born February 11, 1992, in Grand Rapids, Michigan. He lived with his parents and younger sister. The family later moved to the small town of Hudsonville, Michigan.

Taylor was bullied in school for being an actor.

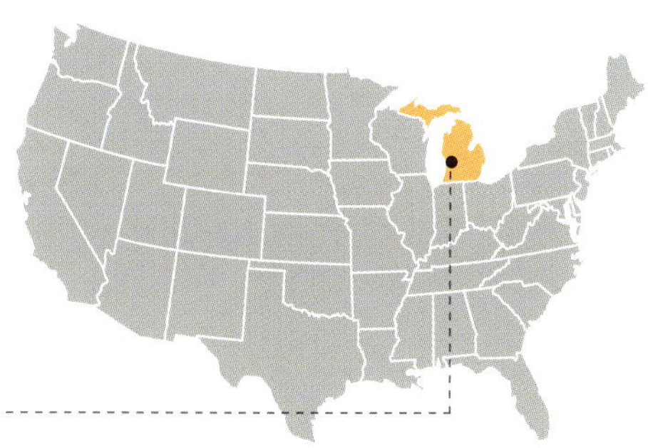

GRAND RAPIDS, MICHIGAN

COLUMBIA PICTURES
TROUBLEMAKER STUDIOS
Kodak
DIMENSION FILMS
Microsoft Windows xp

GETTING INTO ACTING

Taylor loved to play sports like football and baseball. When he was six, he started training in karate. He won three Junior World Championships in karate. Taylor's karate instructor was in many movies. He said that Taylor should become an actor.

Taylor did big flips for the cameras on the red carpet.

Taylor started ***auditioning*** for commercials when he was seven. In 2001, he got a part in the TV movie *Shadow Fury*. The next year his family moved to Los Angeles, California, so Taylor could take more TV roles.

In 2011, Taylor and the cast of Twilight: Eclipse *won an award for the best movie.*

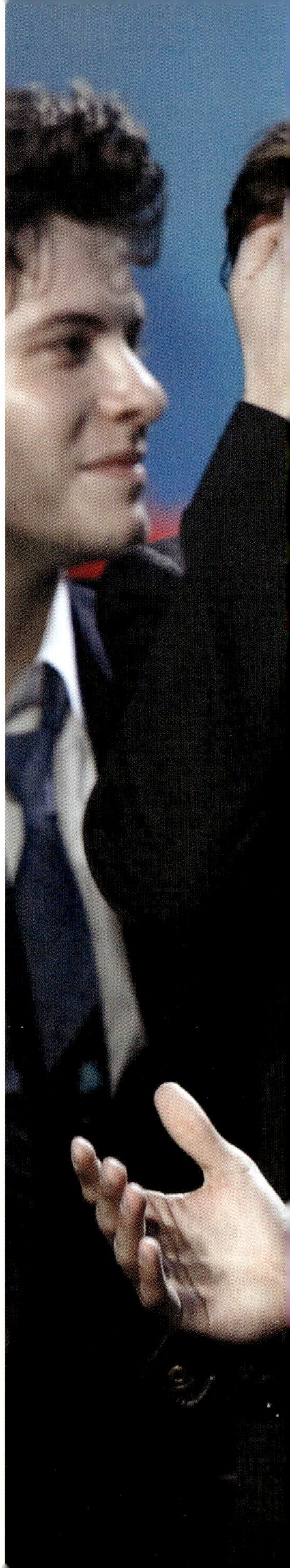

THE BIG TIME

In 2005, Taylor got his first starring role in the movie *The Adventures of Sharkboy and Lavagirl*. Soon, Taylor landed an even bigger part. He played the werewolf Jacob Black in the five *Twilight* movies.

Taylor acted with Kristen Stewart (left) after playing Sharkboy (right).

After *Twilight*, Taylor was **cast** in more movies like *Valentine's Day* and *Abduction*. He did many of his own **stunts** for *Abduction*. Taylor has won many Teen Choice, People's Choice, and Kids' Choice Awards for his acting.

Taylor practiced his own stunts for the 2014 movie Tracers.

LA
The UNIVERSITY OF MICHIGAN

OFF THE SCREEN

When he is not acting, Taylor likes to play and watch football. His favorite teams are the University of Michigan Wolverines and the Detroit Lions. He watches *American Idol*, too.

Taylor wears clothes that show his pride for his favorite sports teams.

GIANT

WHAT IS NEXT?

Taylor planned to make many more movies. He wanted to play different kinds of characters. He also hoped to ***produce*** movies. Taylor's work is likely to keep fans going to the theater for years to come!

Taylor has to stay in shape so that he can do the stunts for his movies.

WHAT TAYLOR SAYS ABOUT ...

CHOOSING ROLES

"It's all based on the story and the character. I want to challenge myself to do many different things."

FANS

"I've had a few girls that have tattooed my signature on their arm. I mean, that blows my mind!"

GETTING STARTED IN ACTING

"I heard, 'No, no, no, no,' so many times. From karate, I had the confidence and drive to push myself."

GLOSSARY

auditioning trying out for a part or job

cast chosen to be in a movie or play

produce to take charge of and pay for the making of a movie

stunts tricks that are dangerous or hard that are done as part of a movie; often, other people perform an actor's stunts so that the actor does not get hurt

WEBSITES

Taylor-Lautner.com

http://taylor-lautner.com/

This site was made by Taylor's fans and has lots of information, pictures, and videos.

Taylor Lautner Biography

http://www.people.com/people/taylor_lautner/

This site has information about Taylor's life and many pictures, too.

READ MORE

Gosman, Gillian. *Taylor Lautner*. New York: PowerKids Press, 2012.

Murphy, Maggie. *Taylor Lautner: Twilight Star*. New York: PowerKids Press, 2011.

Tieck, Sarah. *Taylor Lautner*. Edina, Minn.: Abdo, 2011.

INDEX

PUBLISHED BY Creative Education
P.O. Box 227, Mankato, Minnesota 56002
Creative Education is an imprint of The Creative Company
www.thecreativecompany.us

DESIGN AND PRODUCTION BY Christine Vanderbeek
PRINTED IN the United States of America

PHOTOGRAPHS BY Corbis (MARIO ANZUONI/Reuters, Bowery Boys/Splash News, Paul Fenton/ZUMA Press, Jackson Lee/Splash News, SERGIO MORAES/Reuters, Katy Winn, WUF/Splash News), Getty Images (Chad Buchanan), iStockphoto (Pingebat, Cole Vineyard), Newscom (Rich Kane/Icon SMI 781/Rich Kane/Icon SMI, PacificCoastNews/Newscom, SUMMIT ENTERTAINMENT/Album), Shutterstock (Jaguar PS, Jstone), SuperStock (COLUMBIA PICTURES/Album/Album, SUMMIT ENTERTAINMENT/Album/Album)

LIBRARY OF CONGRESS CATALOGING-IN-PUBLICATION DATA
Bodden, Valerie.
Taylor Lautner / Valerie Bodden.
p. cm. — (The big time)
Includes index.
Summary: An elementary introduction to the life, work, and popularity of Taylor Lautner, an American actor known for his roles in such hit movies as the *Twilight* saga and *Abduction*.

ISBN 978-1-60818-499-6
1. Lautner, Taylor, 1992– —Juvenile literature. 2. Actors—United States—Biography—Juvenile literature. I. Title.
PN2287.L2855B63 2014
791.4302'8092—dc23 [B] 2014000253

CCSS: RI.1.1, 2, 3, 4, 5, 6, 7; RI.2.1, 2, 5, 6, 7; RI.3.1, 5, 7, 8; RI.4.3, 5; RF.1.1, 3, 4; RF.2.3, 4

FIRST EDITION
9 8 7 6 5 4 3 2 1

Note: Every effort has been made to ensure that the websites listed above are suitable for children, that they have educational value, and that they contain no inappropriate material. However, because of the nature of the Internet, it is impossible to guarantee that these sites will remain active indefinitely or that their contents will not be altered.